INTO THE GOOD WORLD AGAIN

POEMS BY

MAX GARLAND

HOLY COW! PRESS
Duluth, Minnesota
2023

Cover photograph (Eau Claire, Wisconsin) by Max Garland.
Author photograph by Lisa Venticinque.
Book and cover design by Anton Khodakovsky.
Lines from Dean Young (1955-2022) are reprinted by permission of his family and Copper Canyon Press, from his forthcoming poetry collection *Creature Feature*, 2024.
Printed and bound in the United States.
First printing, Spring, 2023.

Library of Congress Cataloging-in-Publication Data
Garland, Max, 1950- author.
Into the good world again : poems / by Max Garland.
First. | Duluth, Minnesota : Holy Cow! Press, 2023.
LCCN 2022044378 | ISBN 9781737405108 (paperback)
LCGFT: Poetry.
LCC PS3557.A7162 I58 2023 | DDC 811/.54--dc23/eng/20220928
LC record available at https://lccn.loc.gov/2022044378

ISBN 978-1737405108
10 9 8 7 6 5 4 3 2 1

Holy Cow! Press projects are funded in part by grant awards from the Ben and Jeanne Overman Charitable Trust, the Elmer L. and Eleanor J. Andersen Foundation, the Lenfestey Family Foundation, the Woessner Freeman Family Foundation and by gifts from generous individual donors. We are grateful to Springboard for the Arts for their support as our fiscal sponsor.

Holy Cow! Press books are distributed to the trade by Consortium Book Sales & Distribution, c/o Ingram Publisher Services, Inc., 210 American Drive, Jackson, TN 38301.

For inquiries, please write to: *Holy Cow! Press*, Post Office Box 3170, Mount Royal Station, Duluth, MN 55803
Visit *www.holycowpress.org*

INTO THE GOOD WORLD AGAIN

for Pam and Megan

Table of Contents

III

Some cries never reach us
Even though they're our own.

—Dean Young

No more war, no more plague, only the dazed
silence that follows the ceasing of the heavy
guns; noiseless houses with the shades drawn,
empty streets, the dead cold light of tomorrow.
Now there would be time for everything.

—Katherine Anne Porter, *Pale Horse, Pale Rider*

Riff

For the grit of the ongoing. Not for the sake
of craft, nor deadpan tone of hushed reverence,
nor stylized beat, nor calculated pause, nor
homage to the lack imbedded in the language.
It's nothing you feel called to say
for betterment's sake, nor moral, nor mortal
dept to pay. Not thinly veiled self-regard,
nor humble brag nobody's buying, and never did,
nor righteous complaint, nor any of these excluded,
so maybe it's all of these, all the not's and nor's
welcomed fully back into the fold. For the grit
of the ongoing that only moves by hopeful riff
in search of song, in spite of everything.

I

Intensive Care

If there is a world where all care is intensive,
every symptom deeply monitored, where
the ultimate purpose of math is charting
compassion from chamber
to chamber, this isn't necessarily it.

Money breaks like a wave against us,
grinding itself for the sake of the salt
of some stillness beyond suffering?

Is there, on any of the 300 million worlds
in the habitable zones of sunlike stars,
a planet where it's always your own flesh
and blood on the line, never a stranger
behind the mask?

Where if anyone flinches from the needle
that stings but can't quite find the vein,
the whole field and fabric of being flinches?

And if there's a bright surge in her face,
a comeback of breath now and then,
the whole world is reminded
how brief and timely a spark it takes,
how little kindling the mortal fire
is still willing to work with.

In the Meantime

The river rose wildly every seventh spring
or so, and down the hatch went the town,
just a floating hat box or two, a cradle,
a cellar door like an ark to float us back
into the story of how we drown but never
for good, or long. How the ornate numbers
of the bank clock filled with flood, how
we scraped minute by minute the mud
from the hours and days until the gears
of time started to catch and count again.
Calamity is how the story goes, how
we built the books of the Bible. Not
the one for church, but the one the gods
of weather inscribed into our shoulder
blades and jawbones to grant them grit
enough to work the dumb flour of day
into bread and breath again. The world
has a habit of ending, every grandmother
and father knew well enough never to say,
so deeply was it stained into the brick
and mind. We live in the meantime
is how I remember the length of twilight
and late summer cicadas grinding the air
into what seemed like unholy racket to us,
but for them was the world's only music.

Social Distancing

Distance bears me along in its mobile exile.
—Jules Superveille, *L'escalier*

Say there came a pandemic; some newsdrunk virus
set its hooks in us. And only the sky for a nurse,
arced and empty and barely even blue.

And only the musical pulse, and the several senses
for consolation, except for a stream of distant words
like waves bearing the rush, curl, and foam of elsewhere

arriving, the distant rhythm of others to bridge the gap
between head and heart, dark and day, fear and whatever
it is one feels on the brink of

when walking next to great waters, how the surf catches
and releases the light, and the waves and bones tremble
like the distant cousins of constant thunder.

We know salt tumbles eventually from ocean to body
and back, and forth. We know it takes ages to regather
the shaken self into the good world again.

I remember a ritual once where hundreds of tiny
basket-like boats were lit and launched with prayers
and flowers and misfortunes, ignited and cast out

on the water until the bay was ablaze, a rocking
constellation of human woe uttered in small tongues
of flame, until little by little they drifted, burned,

blinked out, and then it was just dark water again,
and we all went home. Did our troubles never return?
Were we really less burdened, or better people?

What I mean is sometimes worry needs to be ignited,
launched into words, if only to blaze awhile among
flotillas of sorrows we thought were ours alone.

What I really mean, of course, is *Keep in touch*.
Even if you don't know what to say, especially
if you don't know what to say. *Kind words,*

fellow castaways, mind-lit emergencies of fingertip
and tongue, float this festival of downtime and distance,
repopulate the dark with your fledgling human light.

Here in the Amiable Dark

Whatever I want I can outwalk.
—William Matthews

Here in the amiable dark
where we live now, alone
or in couples, or with dogs,

or plugged into music
only one at a time can hear
comes this quelling

above the lethal math of plague
and dearth of love, amid
the new ruins

and ransacked history

where the same familiar beast
with a different mask
is always slouching

above the daily count
of final breaths
we console ourselves

by pretending are not ours,
persuade ourselves are *other*
and *elsewhere*

here in the amiable dark
where we are walking tonight,
the cadence of sidewalks

rising through the circuitry,
climbing the stacked
and loaded dice of the spine

toward the blood rich fields
of the brain, that drenched bouquet
of electro-chemical flowers

which is no more singular
than the mind is singular,
the way reefs and constellations

are never singular, as pity
is never singular
though each holds a portion

trembling in a cup
it's a bottomless cup
we carry

where even walking alone
is never really alone,
whether walking toward

or away from,
there's still *walking*
for company,

and pity and mind
here in the amiable dark
where we live now

Minor Blessing

A neighbor in a red shirt and straw hat
walks his dog into the early day, cigarette
in his right hand, leash in the left,
some sort of terrier. Not a looker.
The leash is a live wire, the dog's world
awash in waves unfathomable to me.

Another summer of pandemic.
Fewer of us are dying, though more of us
are dead. Mortal math never ends well.

On the other hand, leaves are in mid-summer mode,
as lush as they'll get, full-blown, sugar high,
mining the air, cracking the codes
of carbon compounds, casting oxygen
to the wind like giveaway fate.

Linden, maple, catalpa— big green ventilators
over-arching the sidewalks, lawns and houses.

The sort-of-terrier reads the swirling molecules—
currents and eddies within eddies within...

The air is riddled with animal gossip, ripples
with magnified scent. All the lowdown—
who's in heat, who's strange, or missing,
who's dominant? What dug this den?

The air is rich to the terrier's mind, not only
the morning updates, but news from the night before
is scrawled across the grass and tips of junipers.

The terrier doesn't know his owner's shirt is red.
It's more like gray to him, more like smoke,
but he knows its salts and pheromones by heart,
where it's been, nicotine woven into the fibers.

He doesn't know why masks appear, disappear,
and sometimes reappear, but smells the difference.
He's still mildly bewildered by these bonuses
of morning, midday, and late night walks.

Midges are beginning to rise into mid-summer
frenzy. Sex and death in the flower beds,
a loose swarm of ephemeral lust
jiggles above the grassy boulevard,
backlit, translucent.

I like to think something is on the wane,
that this is the week we stumble back
from the brink. Though what I like to think
rarely matters. Other brinks are always arriving,
performances of indignation, monetized rage.

Sometimes what seems like calm
is just the righteous reloading. Even so,

I notice I'm starting to notice again,
register things of minor relevance—a man
in a red shirt and straw hat. A dog, unspectacular,
but intent on *being*, a trail of unleashed
cigarette smoke drifting in their wake.
Trivial, you might say. I might agree.

Except you've have to be alive to say that,
which considering the numbers, is not trivial:
this wasted time, this minor blessing.

Half a Mind

It's hard to know what this sleeping cat wants for himself
except to be safely seen. Right forepaw folded, the left
extended as if in flight. White blaze on an orange face.
God help us. Emergency rooms are full in this town,
fever gurneys floating up and down the hallways.

The latest variant of the virus has vaulted the body
altogether and lodged in the national mind, if a nation
can be said to have a mind. If a mind can be
a makeshift emergency room. I have half a mind
to stretch myself along the bottom of this bed

like the cat, across the quilt sewn from scraps
of family blouses, skirts, neckties and shirts worn
when they were awake and about the business of living.
The mind replicates the body's distress. Or is it
the other way around? How long since I've slept

like that, not *watched over* exactly, but safely *seen*
through the passage from solitude to oblivion
and back? Face ablaze. Right forepaw folded,
left extended as if in flight, as if there were
a place to fly, or a mind not sewn from scraps.

Bedrock

Eau Claire, Wisconsin

We gravitate toward water for the same reason
the rain does—*kinship*. Say you're standing
in the Chippewa River, which is rising,

within and without. You've waded just deep
enough to feel the rush of recent rain, as well
as the reactivated will of ancient rains,

water that split the seed, found the fractures,
and infiltrated the rock, hollowing,
hallowing the valley.

Water is the namesake of this town,
its original and ongoing argument.
Eight pedestrian bridges span the rivers,

but if you think the purpose of the bridges
is to reach the other side, think again, watch
how often people stop halfway across, lean

into the railing, and look—*upriver* for what
they hope might still arrive or *downstream*
for what they thought was theirs to keep,

but now is clearly flowing away, or already
flown, though it lingers into late afternoon
in long swaggering epilogues of light.

If the better part of the planet is water,
and most of the body, and the lungs
resemble sponges left over from the shallow seas

that preceded us, and the brain's natural habitat
is water, as if it were some top-heavy aquatic flower,
briefly marooned on the stalk of the spine,

is it any wonder the mind is awash with longing?

And if everything we see appears to us
through the micro-tide of saltwater and oil
sliding over the cornea, isn't this valley,
this world, *slightly* submerged?

Writing about water is always autobiographical,
ongoing memoir, constantly revised,
from the geysers of the 6th largest moon of Saturn,

to the chemical signatures of water on planets
as far as the infrared lenses of telescopes can reach.
From the swirling confluence of the local rivers

to the wellings of the human heart, which is
part of the watershed, right? Not the oldest part,
nor most enduring, but the *feeling* part.

The main lesson life by water teaches is that *coming
and going are the constant*. No hope of one without
the other, which the heart already knows, of course,

but chooses to forget, though it's inscribed
in the layers of sandstone and shale, recited
by the rapids, even quietly echoed

in the heart itself, chamber by chamber,
atrium and ventricle, memory's deepening echo
all the way down to bedrock.

Footbridge

They're dragging for the boy who jumped into the river,
or possibly fell, or something between the two,
between intent and accident.

The brown river is high and swift. He might be months away.
The cottonwood seeds will drift in what appears to be snow
across the surface. The undercut willows will lean a long time

before they tilt and fall. Kingfishers, like exiled gods,
patrol the varieties of glitter. Even ordinary rocks
in the shallows are beautiful until you hold them,

then duller as they dry, like so much you wanted,
and reached for, and held until the act of holding
evaporated the sheen and lifted the luster.

They will find him a half-mile downriver. All things rise.
Will seal him in black plastic, covered with a white sheet
for our sake; back the ambulance down to the landing.

A *Mastercard* will bear his name. What broke his heart
will remain in the river, on the railing of the bridge, or
in the bar where the lights and music seemed too much,

a kind of exclusion. How we hurt calls for gestures
dangerously close to the brink. In a way, water is a wound
through this town, though in another way

the willows' reflection, the flotillas of cottonwood fluff,
the flash of the kingfisher now and then, are the healing
too. Every footbridge in town, every pause, gaze, thought

launched out into the current, dreams a deeper self.
Possibly his mind changed on the way down. Possibly
how we watch the river is more or less the way he drowned.

The Only Way to Ask

Along the coast of Sheboygan the gulls stand in squadrons
waiting for their shadows to tell them it's time.
I like how they face the wind, some on one leg,
some the other. Early light is cresting Lake Michigan.

Only a radical jogger or two, a woman holding
a coffee mug like a holy icon, a dog walker
with his dutiful plastic glove.

Most of the beach is clear, clean, gradually
waking to light, and the waves, which last night
were ambitious and loud, now tamely collapse,
wash forth, retreat, dimly rattle the sand.

It's the sun spill and spell-binding that hold me here.
No, it's how water goes from platinum to pale shades
of mustard then goldenrod then colors with no names,
and shapes like something alive wants watching
and water is the only way to ask.

Wait, I tell myself, or the brink of day does.
Let the hum of town begin to rise behind you,
the signs on the doors flip from *Closed* to *Open,*
the glass fronts of stores tilt past shadow and silence
toward light the gulls grow restless and hopeful
and loudly rise toward.

A Poem Called Paducah

I was born in a poem called Paducah. Like a coin
or small wave it glittered, like chrome just poured,
polished spoons, or bracelets girls slipped their wrists into.

There was a mile-wide river to float the day upon.
Coal barges churned the deep channel, helping
the big brown water earn its keep.

If I remember correctly, grown men wore hats
and their neckties were bright and broad.
Women rose early to stand behind counters,
or streamed from the hosiery mill
when the whistle sounded, or the Magnavox plant,
or tapped the chalkboard to command our attention.

I rarely remember correctly. Weather vanes
and steeples pierced the semi-permeable sky?
Bibles as bedside ballast when the winds
collided and began to tilt, rotate, and roar?

There were tired hymnals to hold in church.
We plowed the played out fields of the verses,
though occasionally in a chorus, the second
or third time around, an improvised harmony
woke the ghost in the hive, and light
through the windows was briefly honey.

In the words of the poem called Paducah,
vowels opened like morning glories
or the mouths of baby birds. *I like to died*,
my grandmother said, when embarrassed
or surprised, until the night she did.

The day before *Mondee* was *Sundee*,
when we dressed as if for the funeral
of who were the rest of the week.

There were brief spans between wars
and plagues and floods,
like strips of blue through the barn slats.

Radio stations from larger cities
remixed the chemicals inside us
with three minute doses of undying love,
alternating with songs about how love dies.
Painfully, I think it was.

Often I construct a past, I admit, a kind of charm
or spell. Otherwise, it's just here and now
to waft among.

The poem called Paducah assumed the shape
of the river, and everyone recited their breaths
and each pulse rehashed the coming
and going of the world.

At the atomic plant west of town, the tiniest things
were mined for power. Sunset grew rich
through veils of coal ash and steam.

What sort of poem was it then, this town *Paducah*?
It made a percussive sound when you said it.
Strangers smiled when they saw the sign, *wondered*—

maybe guileless, salt of the earth types lived here?
Though life ground their days down to the bone,
they'd give you the shirts off their backs?

It was longer than a sonnet, not exactly an epic,
nor even a *ballade*, this poem, my town.
Composed on the fly, like the gulls above the Ohio
caught currents and updrafts invisible to us,
and off they'd glide with barely a wingbeat.

I still see them sometimes over other cities,
harbors, town dumps, oxbow lakes, or islands
famous for their fineness of sand and rush of longing.

They come to me out of the brilliance, the same gulls,
the hometown metrics of their cries, illuminations
along the edges of their wing feathers
as they descend to the tide line, patrol and pick
among the shattered bracelets of shell and bone
in the backsliding foam,

until the poem called Paducah almost reassembles,
recites itself, rushes home, then unravels
in molecules of salt spray, deep breath,
time and open water.

Near Bailey's Harbor

I've walked this lake for hours, along dolomite
ledges, beside waves wearing crowns of small weeds
winding into pocked pools of algae devoutly
churning sunlight into sugar. Long stretches
of sand from the vast mills of what came before
time was remotely countable, just motion's music.

I've walked to shed the gossip of self, that
unsustainable racket. The reaches of wet light
skimming Lake Michigan are my comely assistants.

A brim of foam fuses each wave. Bare feet leave tracks
so brief the shore barely bothers to register them.
Just shapes that came and went, soon enough sifted
back into the layers with crinoids and trilobites.

Soon enough the breath of air that shaped itself
into the syllables of my name will be elsewhere
and otherwise, wet or blown or weathering the rock
wave by wave into sand for someone else to wander
like a ghost, not unpleasantly along this shore.

Wading the Yellow River

The crayfish scuttle backwards.
They don't like the looks of us,
our big rubber waders, all this uproar of silt.

Give the crayfish a mere shadow to inhabit.
Give them a mossy stone to wear
like a hat or roof.

Claws to snatch a living up.

Give them a gull to fear like God.
A northern pike to pass over
like a portent
of somebody else's doom.

Stealth and hindsight.

Give the crayfish eyes on stalks
like dark aquatic flowers,
a muddy version of a mermaid's tail.

Give them the guts to wear their skeletons
on the outside, where the action is.

They backfling themselves from crevice
to crevice, from the undersides
of sodden branches

curtained with algae,
to the narrows
between frog-spawned rocks.

Grant the crayfish this quick shallow river.
A blesséd mistrust of the human.

An honest grasp of the ghost of a chance.

Morels

You can taste a little of the fountain shaped shadows
of the dead elms in these sliced and sauteed morels,
and taste a little of the grit of the ground down gears
of mid-century America, and a hint of coming home
from the war, and how the atoms hung over us
like God's umbrella, and you can taste
the blue smoke of the chain saws that brought down
the elms, and the iron taste on the tongue
you remember as you sat through childhood sermons
on resurrection, how the meek shall inherit
and so on, and some of the grit of the world
is also in the pan, grain or two of sand, and the years
it took the right rain to call down into the spores.

What's good about the morels is patience
beyond patience. What's good is the wind
that shook the leaves as we strode those streets
under the arched branches of elms and broke
the heart of time and time again, and now
in the taste of morels, brown bread
and body on the altar of the tongue.
Who would have guessed all these years
what small dark churches the shadows
were building, their convoluted steeples
now writhing in salt and butter and oil?

Invasive

Even the zebra mussels who lie here in ruins carved clean,
bleached and rattling in the sand and subtle music of foam,
encrusting the driftwood, even these unloved thumbnails
bear their deaths well in the sun, shorn of whatever nerve

and appetite they harbored, having clung so tightly to sift
their lives from shallow water. Even the misplaced, exiles
borne in ballast, on bowlines, waterweeds and bilge,
claim their foothold in time. Even invaders, cloggers

and corroders, crowding out the local, even the reviled
break down under foot, under time, under wave. Sooner
or later you can't tell the stranded from the strand. Sooner
or later sand and grit gather us up, the mussels and me.

Bone and shell and splintered wood and even ground-down
glass beatified, tumbled time and time again through the gates
of the green waves until even the broken bottle, mindlessly
thrown, assumes the rounded shape of the shining world.

Ocracoke

Once there was a blue sheet of ocean
for life to break upon.

This was morning along the shore
before anyone believed in God
enough to fall from grace.

In the space between one wave
and another, time practiced
her routines—salt in the watchworks,
big wet hours.

Pelicans flew in a quick low line
almost within the curl and blown
foam of the waves.

What were they hunting
or hiding from? Was hunger
already in motion?

Was heartache foretold
in the rattle of broken shells
in the surf?

And what about those hoofprints
sunk in the wet sand?

If you followed them home
would that be a life? Or is life always
where you are already standing?

Something was trying to loosen
the sunlight from the water.

Maybe the wind was involved.

Maybe the surf kept coming apart,
spilling forth, sifting back
through the jack-knife clams
and shattered tellins.

Some of the shells looked like wings
torn from a previous world.

Some of them rang like music
was what they used for money there.

The deeper the listening,
the richer the world.

II

Baby Tooth

There's a tooth beneath your pillow, little one,
though it's not the tooth you lost. A creature of dust

beneath your bed, a strangeness in the closet,
made of wire and shirts and empty coats.

There's a hole in sleep to fall through, barely
ever climbing out of. A dream is you

as much as daylight is, wherever daylight is.
It rounds the world like a rocket.

It might lie down where grandfather
and mother wait like seeds in their furrows.

Shapes in the dark are stirring; that's
the real room you live in—the restless shapes

and the wonderful dark. When a tooth falls out,
they bring you money, yes, but it isn't enough,

and there's still a tooth beneath your pillow,
though never the one you lost.

Carbon

In a dream I saw a table where all the elements fell into place...
—Dmitri Mendeleev

You think the elements know the difference
between the inanimate
and us? And what is the difference, really,
between a rock and the hard place
the human heart becomes, at times?

Does carbon, for instance, *care* if it abides
in coal or bone, pencil tip, French kiss, redwood,
deadwood, double martini, or diamond?

Chimney smoke? Mortal breath?

Do the elements ever miss, like a hometown,
the star of their nativity? Like a manger?
Like we all miss old flames?

Do atoms harbor the memory of immaculate heat,
the way I remember the warmth and rocking
of a mother? Or imagine I do?

Is it accurate to call the outer shell of the carbon atom,
where the latches of the compounds click, *welcoming?*
Or just needy? Or merely tolerant of the prodigal electrons
of hydrogen, oxygen, all the other lost lambs.

Wandering atoms scratching at the door like strays
you let in for the night, who curl at the hearth
and never leave.

Or tiny exiled gods in their sparse garments of motion.

If the elements first flowered outward
like children blow the crowns of dandelions
into wishful scatter and drift, did *we* become,
eventually, their wish come true? So far? Or false?

When the neurons first fired, and thought leapt the synapses
of our separate skulls—was it chemistry or mythology;
evolution or intuition—that first inking of *self*,
like some elemental lamp rubbing itself awake?

If metaphor is the radiant half-life
of an ever-opening mind, *imagine* —

you've been driving all night, through night, beyond
night, drawn by loneliness, or inertia, or gravity.
There is no boredom greater than yours.

And suddenly you see, or think you see something flicker,
like the sputtering *Vacancy* sign of an old motel. Say carbon
is that old motel. One of the early roadside chains.
Carbon 12, let's call it, with two inner rooms always occupied,
and four outer rooms, occasionally, briefly vacant.

And the rooms are time worn, but tidy, the retro
curtains flimsy as ash, and the owner is absent,
but too stubborn to sell, and you've been traveling,
dear wanderer, dear atom, literally forever...

Remember that poem by Frost? The farmer says
home is the place where when you have to go there,
they have to take you in? But his wife says no,
it's more like *something you somehow*
haven't to deserve.

Imagine the carbon atom as that vintage motel, where
when you have to go there they have to take you in.
It's not a matter of *deserve*. Lodge anywhere long enough
and it starts to feel like home, as every immigrant
atom in your body knows.

Mendeleev said he *dreamed* the order of the elements.
It's hard to know for sure. But I do know the right sleep
can take years to fall into— blind alleys, obsessions,
outmoded maps, wrong roads, before the mind stalls
at the limits of logic, and steps out over the edge
for the deep-dive into the sub-structures
and spell-bindings.

Before the right dream turns darkness inside out,
and you see, or think you see, something flicker—*Vacancy*
reconfigured into what, for lack of a better term,
we call *here and now—*
                                    —coal or bone, pencil tip, French kiss,
redwood, deadwood, double martini, or diamond.
The ruse of the material. Chimney smoke, mortal breath,
brief as the distance between darkness and wonder.

Images from Space

Things race away. Even the best of us, the ruddiest,
rolling in dough and dowsing ourselves in adequate
doses of restraint, even the healthy as mules among us

are a blink, a wink or two at best, not even remotely
geological. How long will light grace even the loveliest
eyes? Yours, for instance. Sometimes I can already feel

the hurtling away, the particle winds collectively
howling inside, the bones jittery with calcium
already anxious to be other, to be dismantled

and all earthy again. I can feel the loosening threads
of the fabric of even this thought. My face in the mirror
barely bothers to move as I move anymore.

It's ahead of me, or behind. It's bored
with static resemblance. Things race away. Even
on those planets around those suns in those galaxies

the space telescopes keep harping about, even there,
even on worlds with years that last our lifetimes
even there, things degrade. Light tends to pulse apart

that which it illuminates. I try to remind myself
change is all the real there is. To want otherwise
is to pin the butterfly of being to the wall,

which is good for neither. Still, it's pretty up there.
And time is the only weather worth complaining
about today, this brilliant blue arc

that seems a sky worth forever, but leaks beauty
into the heart wherever I turn, accelerates
the pulse until it can barely be contained.

I mentioned your eyes? That's what I'll remember
when I'm ash, still pouting a little in the breeze
they've tossed me into,

how intensely dark in the middle they were, but the irises
like images from space, those violet gold-flecked nebulae
where better stars are being born.

Instructions for the Outpatient

You may feel a little sting. You may reel
headlong into a breed of darkness
one rarely finds except
in the trenches of major seas.

During the procedure itself
you may have the sensation
of opening like a rare flower.
Bees tremble in the dewy calyx.
This is normal.
They aren't real bees.

The humming originates elsewhere.

Considerable time will pass
during the procedure itself,
though not for you. For you,
it's only a minimal absence,
barely a blink.

Consider yourself
the weight of a feather.
Consider yourself
tucked in the roseate flush
of the extended now.

If it's any consolation, the world
continues without a hitch
in the absence of even the best of us.
This has been proven through time.

As for the sutures, they will vanish
on their own. Where do they go?
We've often wondered.

Where does anything go?—

This world— every field and blossom,
stream and mountain, bluebird
and sea horse, will grow ashen
and blank as the moon in time.
This is not related to your procedure.
This was baked in from the start.

If you should experience undo discomfort,
join the club. *All flesh is grass*,
as the prophet Isaiah once noted.

Should you feel the need to contact us
before your scheduled follow-up,
it's often best to hesitate.
Much is solved by simple hesitation.
Laughter and hesitation.

After approximately three weeks,
most people are able to resume
their normal activities, or abnormal,
as the case may be.

Who are we to judge?

In the meantime, some patients
find warm compresses helpful, or ice.
Others report finding relief in prayer
and common household ointments.
We sincerely hope you are among them.

Finally, try not to pick at the wound.
It's hardly ever where you think.

Long Haul

Worn out, worn down, whittled away, neither
exploded nor imploded, but the will eroded
in runnels and rivulets, in quiet sweeps
of second hands.

Neither blind-sided by cloud burst
nor thunder clap, but brain-fogged,
mind veiled, cataracted
by a high gauze of altostratus
where clarity of thought should be.

Not absolutely devoured, but nibbled away at,
nickeled and dimed. No full-blown conflagration,
but this constant low-grade fever,
this whispered gossip of kindling.

Not completely gone, but faintly absent,
the bodily cells flaking away
like the dried out petals of get-well bouquets.

How calendars feel when you look at them
now—sheepish, like they know the linear
is a lie, that time moves no longer
in patient procession, but Dopplered
into ever lengthening throbs of distance,

the days of the week having forgotten
the gods they were named for,
but still willing to pass the plate,
as if even the little of you left to give
might be almost enough to matter.

The Only Person You've Spoken To Today

You almost forget how words work,
where they come from and go and why.

If they'll ever return, and to whom?

Your hands are washed so far beyond clean
it might be the afterlife already. Sanitized

deeper than skin, down past the blue ropes
of vein and braided muscles, into the marrow

of the 27 bones, those artful shards.
Soap is your hobby now.

From beneath your grocery mask, dog-
walking mask, drive-in window mask,

you aspire to words you hope are kind,
kindling, conspiratorial, marginally

curative? At least beyond perfunctory.

But when the masked high school girl
behind plexiglass at the register at Kroger

says *Have a Blesséd Day,* a phrase you've
never uttered to another human being,

You, too is all you come up with, mumbled
into your own mask, as if by some miracle

she'll know that you know, *Don't die*
is what you both mean.

I Just Kept Driving

Sometimes I drove for days without so much
as a minute passing. Other times the minutes
held days the size of stars.

I sang to myself as I drove.
The sun in full retreat. The race
of the blue-black thunderhead.

There was radio news. Children toted Kalashnikovs.
A young woman taped a bomb between her breasts.
God whispered terrible commands.

I drove until the wheat gave way to little pines
and bedrock started to show on the hills. Sumac,
patches of lupine. I think it was bedrock.

I drove as if to steady myself, or ready
myself, whichever came first. Time hurt,
the way it lodged in the undone

and all too soon undoable. I'm backsliding,
I thought, remembering the Baptists. All I need
is a gilded river and a dove to glide down in Greek.

All I need is to be sewn back into the garment
of the sensible world. I just kept driving,
like the scene of the crime trying to leave itself.

Rain came in slanted sheets.
The radio stuttered something
that seemed only remotely possible.

I felt slightly aloft, possibly hydroplaned
a mile or more. Then either the rain stopped
or I sang to the other side. I noticed

the world had begun to blur
into a kind of distant beauty,
the lethal kind. I just kept driving.

But I was no longer myself by then,
the landscape shook loose like a ribbon,
and the road was just wind.

Dubious Stars

It's strange how hard we fought to grow old
and once arrived, wanted none of it.
How they prodded and probed, sliced away
the withered parts. How marvelous their gadgetry.

And still the recalibrated heart pumped dismay
onto the bigger and balder-by-the-year brow.
The eyes worried like fish in their sink holes.
How we drank to our health, jogged through slush

when even the sparrows kept to the evergreens,
what with the nip and sudden throttle
of March wind, and now the very skin
we stroked like money, sought to preserve,

seems randomly splotched and riddled
as if scrawled by a drunken cartographer—
too much rum and laudanum in the hold
of his ship too long at sea, all those months

of clattering gulls, hardtack and over-salted cod.
Maybe I'll paint some islands here, he thinks,
a storm swept ridge, a skein of varicose
rivers branching away.

Strange, how clocks run the night down now,
our blessings so bountiful we can't sleep for counting
them, like sheep on the hills of the old country,
or the dubious stars that steered us here.

What's Left For You to Say?

Light traveled a long way for this.
Wracked the white hot heart of the sun,
tore itself away just in time
to slide through the blinds, grace
the window sill of Room 412.

Flowers the church people brought
are starting to wilt.

The patient's right arm is a bad map
of bruises. The left, another map.
The blue cartography of an inside job.

Under a thin gown, the rhythms of inhalation
and exhalation are not well matched.

Gown—as in graduation, wedding,
ballroom gown; as in Rita Hayworth,
Diana Ross, Beyoncé
at the never-ending *Grammys*.

Here the ghost of glamour unravels.
There's a glitch in the mortal estuary,
a pulse more ebb than flow.

Intubation, mobile morgue, protein spike
are all the news, but there's still
just plain old death, the kind
that always happens,

where hypoxia steals the brain's
best lines, substituting older scripts.

Occasionally, the previous dead walk
right rudely into the room, which
the patient no longer mentions.
Why bother?

The flesh is a gown, you guess, the heart
its corsage, worn on the inside, oddly enough,
petals spilling down and down.

It took a hundred thousand years for light
to wrangle its way from the center of the sun
to the brink of the window sill,
and adorn the particulars of this room—

IVs and monitors, railed bed, bad chair,
high tilted soundless TV where
the 7th season of *Friends*, Episode 14,
"The One Where They All Turn Thirty,"
is much more eloquent without sound.

Math flashes across a bedside monitor.
Something about incoming and outgoing,
a human tide chart.

It turns out the pulse has a fleeting sense
of where it belongs, and to whom.

It turns out the hydrogen atoms
at the center of the sun collide so madly,
they embrace each other inside out,
their fusing so torrid the spin-off
is *this*—

this slag of earthly light, this world
enough and time to watch the one
you've loved the longest raft away.

Don't you mean *waft* away?
Does it matter?

The skin is a gown.
The day is a gown.
The light is wilting
on the window sill.
Math is spilling its
petals down and down.

What's left for you to do?
How much does the long
suffering light allow?

Oh Rachel. Oh Ross.
It's extremely mortal here.
What's left for you to say?
Oh Joey, You're right.
Silence is a gown.

What Clouds the Mind with Love

I recognize this bar by the smell of the lack of purpose
here, and how maybe there's more to the mirror
than meets the eye. Say you're perched on one
of the planet's many bar stools, and here comes
an absolute flame of a person. I mean here comes truth
and beauty with a timely amount of local swagger,
and the bottles behind the bar are arranged
like cathedral spires but the choir is mostly internal,
a series of flashes from the hot ends of dendrites
and you're possibly passably articulate enough
to look him or her in the eye and say, you don't
know me, but much that you do know is also known
to me, the sky, for example, and the stars therein.
It's almost as if we're two creatures fashioned
for the same dark destination. In the meantime,

what are the odds?—this very world,
the emergence of life forms, the invention of speech,
the rise and fall of etiquette, the buzz in the brain
that binds us as sisters and brothers, and yet
the crucial estrangement that mimics the distance
between one fingertip and another, that mirrors
in turn all distance, both within and without, and yet
here we are, in the fleeting attire of flesh and blood,
as the mirror pearls the dim grit of the room, as if
the past were drunk and gone, and the future
possibly illegal, which, correct me if I'm wrong,
is what strips the gears of clocks and stars,
and clouds the mind with love.

Cardinal Cardenalis

> *...The cardinal*
> *who lives beside the redbud, he whose crimson*
> *is richer than that pink, he who almost*
> *shames the tulips, he whose carnal cry*
> *is always loud and florid, he is my witness.*
> —Gerald Stern, "The Ukrainian"

There's a redbird who hates me so
he cracks open sleep most mornings
as you lie right beside me, though
the distance is vast,
like those voyages we studied in school,
the sea routes traced on fanciful maps.

The four winds had faces with puffed
up cheeks. Leviathan lurked here
and there among the cartoon waves.

Love is as strange as the world,
as provisionally charted,
as embellished with omen.

The sun sears the bedroom blinds, yet
that never wakes me, nor do the tectonic
shiftings of the old house, nor the crack
of dawn dog-walkers with their sleepy urgings,
commands, and precious bags of crap.

But he hates me, the redbird, in the needle-
blighted spruce, in the silver maple, the way
he hammers and pries— three notes,

then four, a watery backfill, a finishing flurry,
then a pause

through which I begin to drift,
though not to sleep, then the sequence
replays itself, but more piercing
this time, more irrevocable.

He's a lit coal tapering into flame.
He's the furious soul of the lesser trees.

I try to work his song into the rhythm
of my own breath, or yours—*rise, fall*—
but he switches times, each note a jolt,
not lethal, but in the ballpark.

I look at you, your sleeping face, curves
and bones and breath, slight twitch
of lashes, lips at peace.

He's after love, I think, the redbird,
and sometimes there's a faint answering call.

But mostly it's just—*I'm here, I'm here*—
that insistent song of naked presence
as clear and sharp as shards of water
hammered into the early light, as I lie beside you,
though the distance is vast as a voyage we never
studied in school, and I've drifted, not to sleep,
but off the map, and only the redbird knows why,
just you and the redbird.

To Be Alive With You

I'd wreck my heart to have you, my only heart,
my lump in the chest, bump in the night, thump
and rattle against the calcium cage of the ribs.
I would crack it like a favorite cup, this heart.
Wring it like a washrag. Though to *have* you
is wrong, I know. A love is let go
or not love at all. I learned that from sonnets,
or the Beatles, or Sting, or possibly the Bible.

That it's wrong to *have* you also wrecks my heart.
Either way we're goners. That's in the Bible, too.
That may *be* the Bible. We're nailed upon the bones,
a thump or two above the dirt. This dirt I wreck
with barely breath enough to be alive with you—
my heart's glad rattle, my cage, my broken cup.

Why Ancient People Went Out of Style

It was the lead in the pottery, or the flea in the rat's fur.
It was the ash cloud stalled over the sun or the lack
of proper toiletries. It was the worm in the heart
the radium in the well, the tainted run-off,
the meteors thrown over the shoulder of the dark
like flaming bridal bouquets.

Some of the ancients couldn't adapt, and some
adapted beyond all means of detection, like the soul.
It was the lack of penicillin, but nevertheless
the burning desire. It was the jealousy of the gods,
the invention of the catapult, the gnawing of enemies
down past the bone and into the marrow.

It was the boring literature, the ill-fitting tunics,
the conflicting commands from burning shrubs
and dreams and the livers of sacrificed sheep.
It was the wear and tear of trying to remember
which age you were even *in*—

Early Woodland or High Medieval? Late Coptic
or Tang Dynasty? And did it really feel like,
say, the Bronze Age when you were actually *in* it,
digging a root or breathing on a flame?

It was the ravaging and pillaging. The cycle
of surplus and shortfall. The vibrating tymbals
of the periodic cicadas weakening the tender
seams of the infant skulls.

It was the viral pursuit of happiness, the perfection
of the clenched fist and jaw and mind. The dazzling array

of purges combined with the planned obsolescence
of the moment at hand.

It was the increasingly telegenic mobs and updated
plagues with their tiny, protein grappling hooks
ripping the pink sails of the lungs apart,
disrupting the supply chains of breath, combined
with the unchecked fevers that melted the wings
of the last indigenous angel of metaphor. Then
the idioms and wardrobes began to unravel
and we all just ran out of heartbeats.

III

Song for the Worm

Plow forth, little worm. No star
for you till spring. Dive deep
and eyeless with your five hearts
hidden where frost can't find.

Under footfall, under lichen
and liverwort, under the planet's
curve, tucked into the shadow
of the wobble.

In tiny arenas of ganglion
dream up time from scratch
and snow melt, from stirrings
of the eventual. But not now.

Now is no time. Plow down.
Let bleakness be not resisted,
but undermined, little worm.
No star for you till spring.

The Mouse

The Ohio River kept the world at a distance,
nearly divine. Morning carried the smell of mud
and diesel, bleat of coal barges locking through.
Tufts of cottonwood and willow catkins
rimmed the waterline.

Beyond the steel lattices of the mile-long bridge
lay Illinois, which meant *North*,
and from there on to the great blue boxes of cities
where the men who ran things pulled their levers.

But there was no crossing the river without dead-
dragging home behind—caved-in creekbank,
brick thick Bible, the habit
of hunkering in the presence
of whatever glittered godlike and won.

Blesséd are the meek, the mild, the meager,
the field mouse who crept from behind the stove
each night, slinked the baseboard of the trailer
to the bathroom sink where he nibbled
away the corners of the *Ivory* soap,
sometimes even into the name.

Blessed are the hungers, the small and gray
and soft of step, the hardly a whisper.

Sometimes I watched the Ohio River
as if watching a god, or the hem
of god's garment, or a moat,
or a broad green endlessly woven will
from which the frayed thread of my own was torn.

There is another world, I knew from hymns
and headstones. We sang it so in church,
saw it prefigured in backwater fog, the soup
of sloughs, the rising steam of Sunday dinner,
murmurations of starlings winding
over the river to roost.

After dark we heard transmissions from
the other world—the quick-fire static
of radio interference, bleed
of northern accents overriding
our local announcer's drawling
late night weather.

At bedtime I knelt, blessed whatever
blood relatives I could name, blanket-
blessed the rest, prayed we not
be burned alive, or vaporized
too soon, then floated out
into the dark, or half-floated,
half-floundered, as the trailer walls
ticked and rustled, and the river ran on
without mercy, or malice, or rest,
while the mouse climbed his sink pipe,
and sank his teeth into the soap.

Remembering Grace

You *recited* grace
through the rising steam
of supper bowls—*Kentucky Wonders*
laced with bacon fat, potatoes beaten
to a goodly froth.

And you *received* grace
through the brief death of God
back in Bible days
before the holiness in things
grew silent.

A cloud might call your name
back then. A flaming shrub.
The dreams of the pure in heart
were thick with oracular angels.

You bore *disappointment* and *defeat*
with the grace of the good cowboy.
Grace was the lushly painted sunset
you rode hard luck toward.

Manners and clean hands
were second cousins of grace.

Singing a *third above* another voice
created a tremor of grace,
a tympanic buzz in the holy
bones of the middle ear.

Grace was more than the sum
of its parts. Grace was more
than you deserved,

given the shadow self, nested
deep within the self
that wore the light of day.

You could *fall* from grace
a long dark way, and land
in a place, if you landed at all,

where the cruelest thing
was not what you endured
nor even imagined,
but what you *remembered*
of grace—the steam
and the rising appetite,

the tremor in the skull.

They Used to Name Children That Way

The Bible lay on the living room table or else
wind might lift the house like a leaf or the dust
from which we came and duly returned.

A religious sheen to the table top, like still water
upon which our reflections dimly appeared. Bored,
I'd open the Bible at random to air out my fate.

The pages smelled like a very old Valentine
from a boy my grandmother once loved, I guess.
Smelled like Solomon's shoes. Smelled like the pockets
of coats no one wore, nor had the heart to throw away.

... the cart came into the field of Joshua, a Bethshemite,
and stood there, where there was a great stone:
and they clave the wood of the cart, and offered
the kine a burnt offering unto the Lord

They used to name children that way, opening the Bible
and blindly darting a finger down— *Joshua, Beth.*

I imagined my own family someday—spunky kids
I'd whip into shape to weep and remember me by
when I was dust borne up to the Lord.
How they'd sit in this very room, still as mice,
and their generations after them—*Carter, Clave, Kine*—
all the way to the end of the long afternoon.

The Dead Will Rise from Their Caskets Like Painted Eggs from Easter Baskets

Something is hovering, or possibly hunkering,
or maybe hungering to come forth as you float
through the sermon waiting for time
to return. Grandfather sleeps at your left shoulder.
Grandmother wears a hat and veil for the Lord
temporarily slain for us. Nylons whisper
when a grown woman two Christians
down the pew, crosses her legs, swings the toe
of her high heel up and down. Like the mind
moves up and down. You can hear a lot
from the sides of your eyes. Only you
and God know what. Sometimes
you make up rhymes to hide inside.

The way sand in sunlight sifts through
your fingers? The woman's nylons
sound like that. The pointed toe of her shoe
swings up and down at odds with the point
of the sermon, you suspect. The Gospels
are glass to see through darkly. The feathers
of doves shall brush them clean in time.
The body of the Lord tastes like broken crackers,
Saltines, in fact, but holy just the same.
His blood has notes of Concord grapes.
In a shot glass at the altar, you down the juice
like cowboys in saloons wash dust away.

You can read in the polished grain of the pews
the story of when they were living oaks
and wind ran through the fingered leaves
like sand, like the woman's legs crossing

and uncrossing. He died on a cross,
did Jesus, which had once been a tree
a child might climb in a better world.
In a better world, this church might be
some green expanse— meadowlark, quail,
soft wind through thigh high grass,

and now again the sound of sifting, whispering,
the toe of the woman's shoe up and down
like the mind moves up and down
in a different time than the preacher's words,
which are not even words by now, just sliding
waves of consonants, and you, *dear boy,*
your shoes just able to scrape the floor,
marooned hip deep and rising
toward the mouth of the missing vowels.

Looking After

—for Melvia Jean Garland

The bees were counting on us not to kill them,
but nobody's perfect. And also the pandas
and sunflower sea stars and grandparents,
not to mention the frogs in the lovely muck
of marshes, and wrens of the underbrush.

Such an intricate ordeal, untying the knot
of self. And then to find how far the self
expands beyond her former borders.

Who will nurture a mind worth half the time
it took to construct the orbits of atoms
and corral the particles into memory
enough to house the hum of the world
in spite of the sting, the wear and tear?

Who will treat this world, the beaten waves,
smoldering woods and blue cleavings of ice,
the way the oldest proverbs command
all wanderers be treated?—

Shake out the sheets. Dust off the good plates.

Bless his heart, my mother might have said
of a rain-drenched dog, or redbird dazed
by the window glass. Which I understood
was a tender command
that something needed *looking after*
for an hour, a day, as long as we lived?

63

Who will treat this world the way her god
insisted we treat the drenched, bedraggled,
estranged and strangely familiar
whose hurt was ours until it was over?

Tranquility

A month after his funeral she forgets what the hooks by the living room door mean. Why the birds cling to the branches of the crape myrtle outside the window like ornaments the kids forgot to put away. A month after the funeral the car is locked deep in the garage. The sidewalks rolled back like ribbons onto the gray spools that spawned them.

So many gadgets around the house. Touch one and static snows across a screen. Touch another, and... *nothing*. Press a button on the one her daughter labeled *THIS ONE* and there's an flurry of sub-human racket. A studio audience screams in delight or terror. Odd, she never noticed the terror before. Mostly she leaves the gadgets, like sleeping dogs, where they lie. They're not what hands are for.

The dead are allowed to drift back from the vale of temporary consolation, she discovers. But not for long. They have their own work, she guesses. Hauling the moon from phase to phase. Ornamenting the night grass with small wet beads.

The mind is a web things fly clean through. Others catch on the silken grid, vibrating the strands. The mind is the work of an elderly spider. More wriggles free than catches anymore. Either they were married for 68 years or 86, or a day and a night. Of that much she's certain.

Now she remembers what the hooks by the door are for. *Coats*. I was a green coat, she thinks. He was a blue one. But the third hook? A breeze moves through the crape myrtle just outside. Possibly the third hook is for that?

She decides she will drive somewhere, though the car is vaulted deep in the faraway garage, and her license expired years ago, her knees are bone on bone. Was it a dream she ever drove?

For all she knows they've tangled the roads in knots by now. Her children are old and tricky, have probably hidden the keys in a drawer too low for her to reach, among expired medicines, Emery boards, snarled string, extra batteries for the gadgets.

The birds wait along the branches of the crape myrtle in the yard. If you press the right button on the right gadget they might remember how to rise.

He does drift back down to her sometimes, though he never speaks. Words are for amateurs. It's more like the down-drift of dream—the two of them young and nearly breathless in the back seat of the sedan he borrowed, or said he did. All those years ago.

Cars were bigger then. The moon was bigger, though more distant before anybody walked there. A small woods miles from town where the moon spilled down through hickory trees is where they hid. She wishes she remembered the name of that sea where the astronauts landed on the moon; not a real sea, of course. A pretty name.

It was a quarter-moon their first night in the woods. A rutted dirt road where a house had been, but only trees now to close over and hide them. Back seats were big as beds then. A weight lifted, then lightly fell, then lifted again.

They were off the map. Out of the world. *Kids,* she thinks. *Stupid,* she says out loud. The quarter moon breathed for them until their own breath came back. The moon was a hospital. The last night she ever saw him was in the hospital. He was moon pale. Barely breathed. Hardly a ripple on the heartbeat machine.

She thinks she might drive there if they haven't cut the woods, if the car can be roused back to life. All keys are somewhere. All doors roll open if you press the right button on the right gadget.

Maybe the third hook by the door is for the coat the moon pulled over them as they lay in the car the night they eloped, heads and hands full of something like a *dare*. There's a time for losing and a time for finding, she's pretty sure the Bible still says. If I try every gadget in this house, one will surely drive the knots loose from the road, find the woods, force the moon to spill back down over them. *Elope us, again.*

When the birds remember their missions the car will surely start. Key or no key, she'll find the woods. They can't have cut them all. It will be like the blue weight of his coat lifted, then falling, then lifted through the branches back up to the moon hooked over them. The astronauts took a picture of earth from that moon, the world barely bigger than a water bead on a grass blade.

Possibly, she embroidered the moon onto the memory. Maybe it was just plain dark in the woods and the moon stands for the glare of *after*, the outrage of her mother and father, the light of consequence once they were found out, *stupid kids* eloped in somebody's car, tucked under an imaginary moon. Sixty-eight years? Or 86? A day and a night?

Too many tricky turns to drive there now, even *if* the key, even *if* the car. Even *if* the garage door groaned open like the grave, the world would not be the same pretty bead, she bets.

What she never tells the children, those gray-haired semi-strangers, is the most important thing. She looks *forward* to the time when the holes in her mind are completed. There's a system, like a tide. Rising quietly over the details. Stranding the keys in the beaks of birds on the myrtle branches. Memory is more like poetry than memory. Something like that.

She hopes the holes in her mind are finished soon. Her children are kind, but forgettable. *He* was the notion I never shook, the motion that strung me like a bead, she thinks, knew me like a nerve.

She hopes the work is hard in Heaven. She wouldn't mind the distance if the dead were well employed; it would suit him, she thinks, that his hands may not be idle, nor empty as her own.

The Dolphins

There is no distance finer than love. It's nestled
in the skull just above the shell of my left ear.
When I was ten, I paddled a styrofoam surfboard
much too far out in the Gulf. No real surf, just
small waves never-ending. More like ripples
in a blue-green scarf. A pod of bottle-nosed dolphins
rose between the shore and me, arced with a motion
like sewing themselves in and out of the sea,
like stitching a seam between me and the shallows.
The thrill of imagined wildness, being briefly
on the other side. My parents small and strange,
distorted by the heat-rippled air above the sand.

Father waving both arms. Mother's hands cupped,
calling something I pretended not to hear. I was
the boy they'd lost at sea, the son the dolphins stole.
All water would remind them of this forever, every spray
of rain, hillside spring, every brimming bowl. There's
no distance finer than what you wish you'd known sooner,
swam home and said, salt in your hair. I've known people
who boast of having no regrets, but I don't trust them.
Mine taste like salt, move in small remembered waves
like this, unimportant and never-ending.

A Poem of The Late Cenozoic

The times were hard to know when we were in them.
It's afterwards the labels seem to fit— *Stone Age,*
Byzantine, Middle Kingdom, the Nixon Years.

But when we were *in* them, the years were just one after
another, mere morning and night, the squall
of an infant, a crow crying or barking, then the cries

of the other crows, not all that unlovely once you catch
the cadences, begin to notice the oily iridescence
of the feathers, violet and blue, how their flight

is more swimming than flying, how they choose
the most melodramatic branches of the white pine, walk
like sentinels along the ridges of the neighbor's roof.

But the times as we *lived* them were not yet assembled
into meaning. The sun rose, sure, but that's just
a figure of speech, nor does the morning

actually *begin.* Morning and night are nothings
the planet passes through on its way around.
The sun never knows if it's Tuesday or Monday,

nor which of the last few shopping days
it illuminates. As far as the sun is concerned
it might as well be one of those days on Venus

that lasts longer than a year, or one of Jupiter's
ten-hour days, or possibly high noon of the last day
which is always arriving.

But once the times are *over* we know them by name,
grow misty at their very mention—Oh, *the Sixties*, we moan.
How tidy the *Edwardian Age*. How sepia tinted

the latter moments of the *Great Depression*, we note.
And what about the *Middle Ages, Ming Dynasty, Late
Paleozoic* or *Space Age*? What about *The Year We Met*?

When they happen it's just one wave after another,
a little foam, backsliding of surf, at best a cluster
of latent joys implanted for the later flowering.

At the moment, it's just one word after another,
and the longer the intervals between them
the more awkward the air. Though later,

the gaps will seem to have been
where all the meaning was, the spaces
between words where we most deeply lived.

Afterwards we will name them the *Dreamtime*,
the *Axial Age*, the *Great Pandemic*, the *Insurrection*,
though they were all just minutes and hungers, fears,

pulse after pulse and funeral pyres, baby teeth
tucked under pillows, harmless lies we told the children
who told theirs in turn, and then one day we look back,

and *yes*, we insist, it *was* shaped just like that, shone like that,
uniformly defined. But when we were *in* them, *were* we infused
with knowing, or belonging? *Was* reason was all the rage? *Did*

angelic presences haunt the steel gray dawns? At the moment,
there's a lumber train bleating along the ridge above the river.

71

The crows are quiet. There's racket in the mind, but the talk

between us is just this and that, mundane, gossipy.
Everything we say means something else, of course,
but that's not news anymore, if it ever was. It's very cold;

the snow resembles suspended wingbeats along the roofs
of the houses. *When We Were Together* we'll name this era,
remembering the stiff white wings of the houses.

But at the moment there's just a little tension, the ordinary
tilt of the earth away from the sun, hexagons of frost
on poorly insulated windows, the year almost over,

the world locked in the groove of elliptical orbit, domestic
particulars—books, plates, strewn clothes, rumpled beds.
A few miles from here, citizens in blaze orange are perched

at the edges of stubbled fields, triggering the distance between before
and after. It's not any age at all, nor era, nor does the bullet know
it's bound for the left shoulder of the buck, or doe, nor does

the year know it's winding down, nor does the *Millennium*
know its name, nor does the blood pulsing from atrium
to ventricle and down the digital arteries to the fingertips know

it's riffing toward "*A* Poem of the Late Cenozoic" nor its major
themes and many digressions, nor where in mirth, or mire, the line
or poem or age will end.

Acknowledgements

I'm grateful to the editors of the following publications in which some of these poems first appeared.

"In the Meantime"—*Academy of American Poets*, poets.org, Poem-a-Day

"Song for the Worm", "Tranquility", "What Clouds the Mind With Love"— *Barstow and Grand*

"Bedrock"— *MdW Atlas*

"Social Distancing"—*Singing in the Dark, A Global Anthology of Poetry Under Lockdown*

"Baby Tooth"—*Volume One*

"Carbon"—*Wisconsin People and Ideas*

About the Author

MAX GARLAND is the author of *The Word We Used for It,* winner of the Brittingham Poetry Prize. Previous books include *The Postal Confessions,* winner of the Juniper Prize, and *Hunger Wide as Heaven,* which won the Cleveland State Poetry Center Open Competition. He has received an NEA Poetry Fellowship, a Michener Fiction fellowship, inclusion in *Best American Short Stories,* and fellowships in poetry and fiction from the Wisconsin Arts Board. Born and raised in Kentucky, where he worked as a rural letter carrier on the route where he was born, he is Professor Emeritus at University of Wisconsin-Eau Claire, and the former Poet Laureate of Wisconsin.